Who Am I?

Sir Sidney Poitier

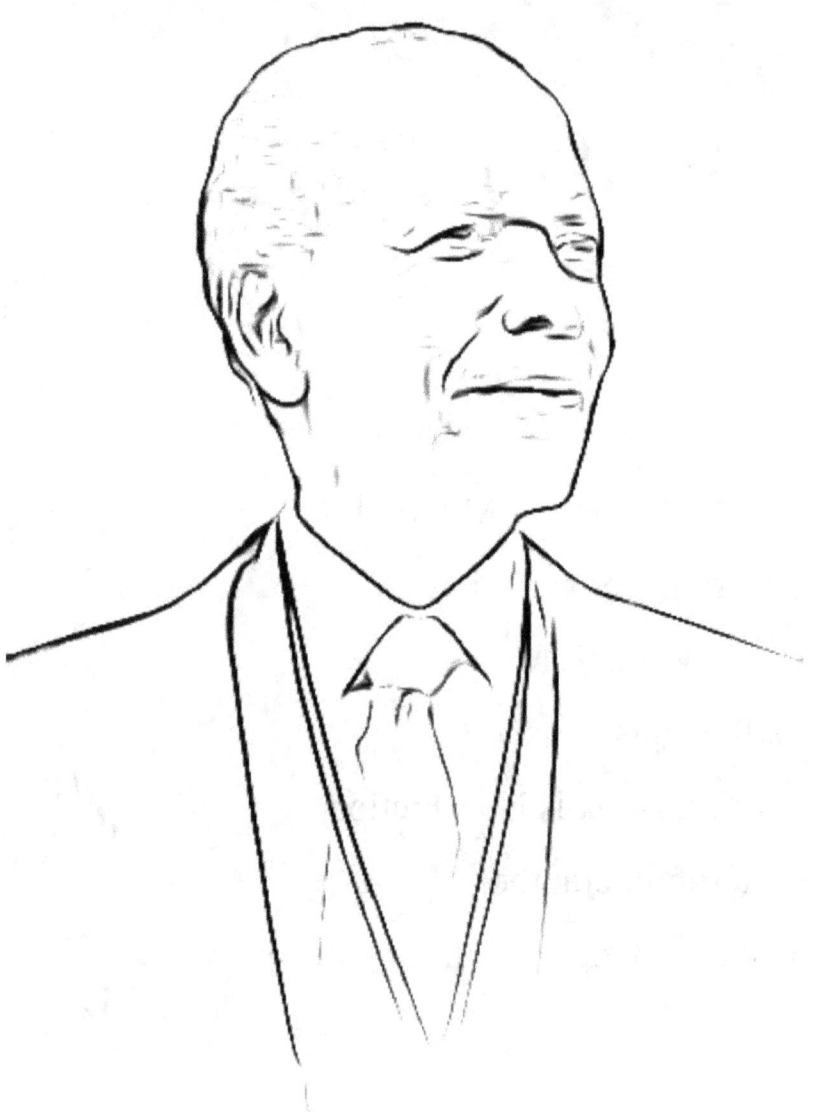

I am an actor, author, diplomat, and film director. I won an Academy Award for "Best Actor" becoming the first African American to win this award. I currently serve as the Bahamian Ambassador to Japan.

Jackie Robinson

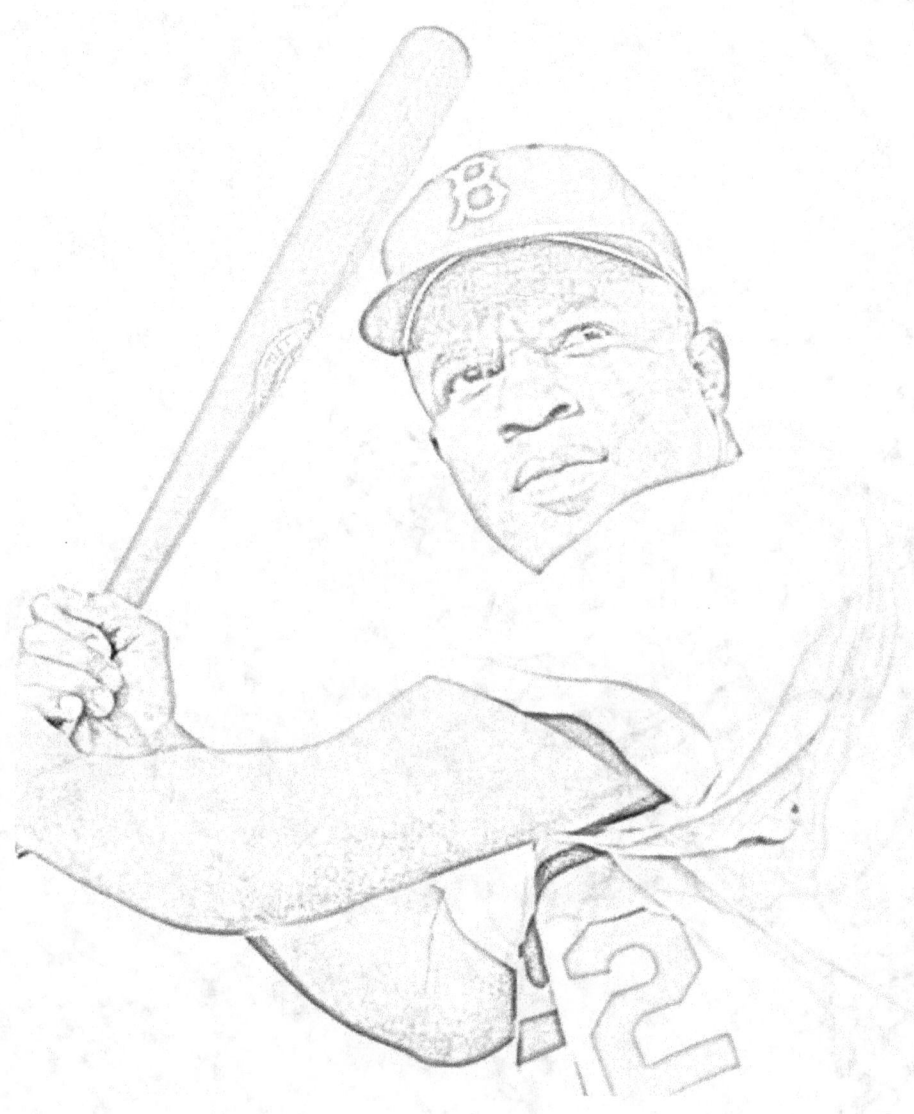

I was a Major League Baseball (MLB) player and played second base. I was the first African American in the MLB. In 1947, I was rookie of the year.

Marian Wright Edelman

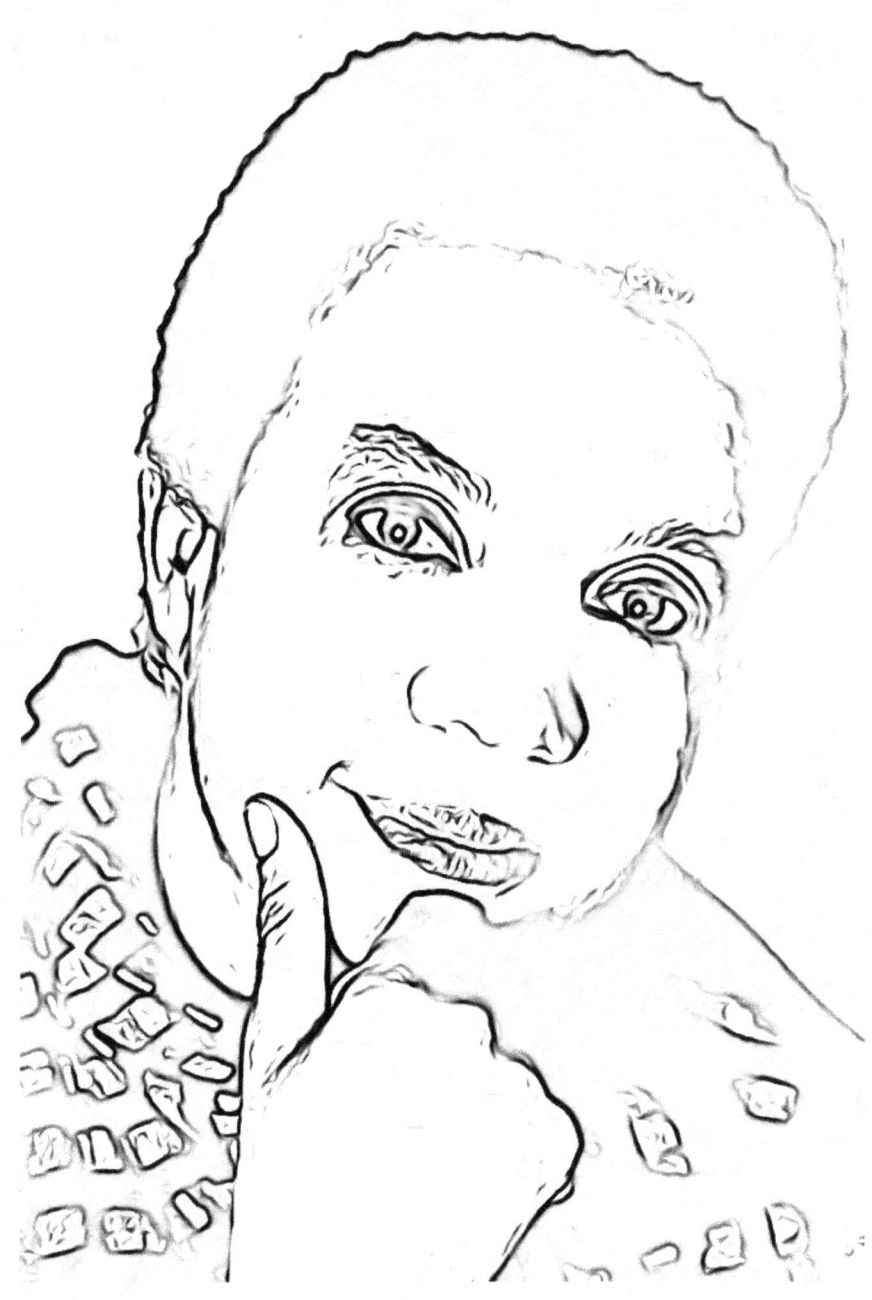

I have been an activist my entire life. I was the first African American woman admitted to the Mississippi Bar and was the founder and president of the "Children Defense Fund."

Elizabeth "Bessie" Coleman

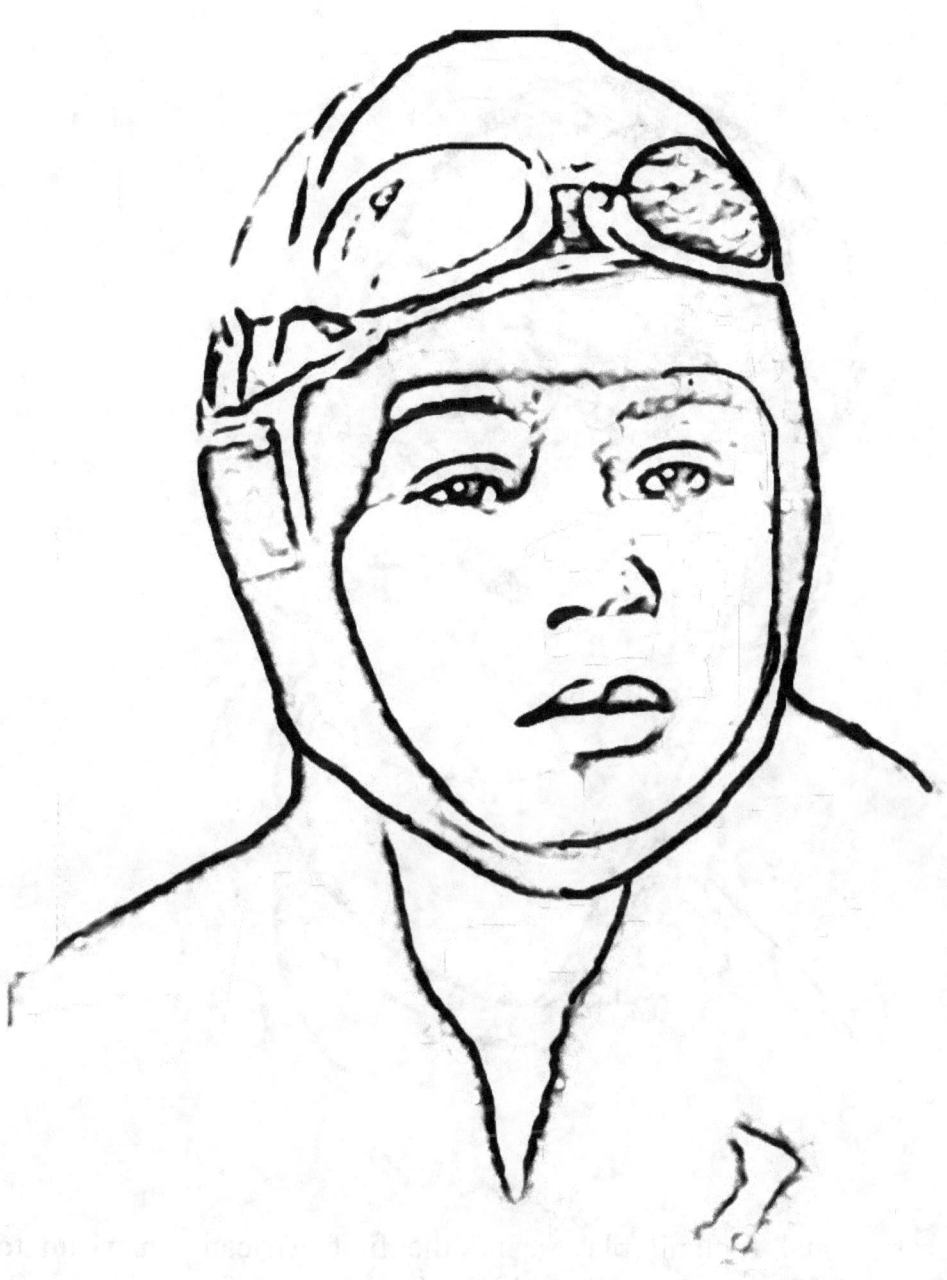

I was a civil aviator and became the first African American licensed woman pilot. I became a stunt pilot and had a career in exhibition flying

Kenny Washington

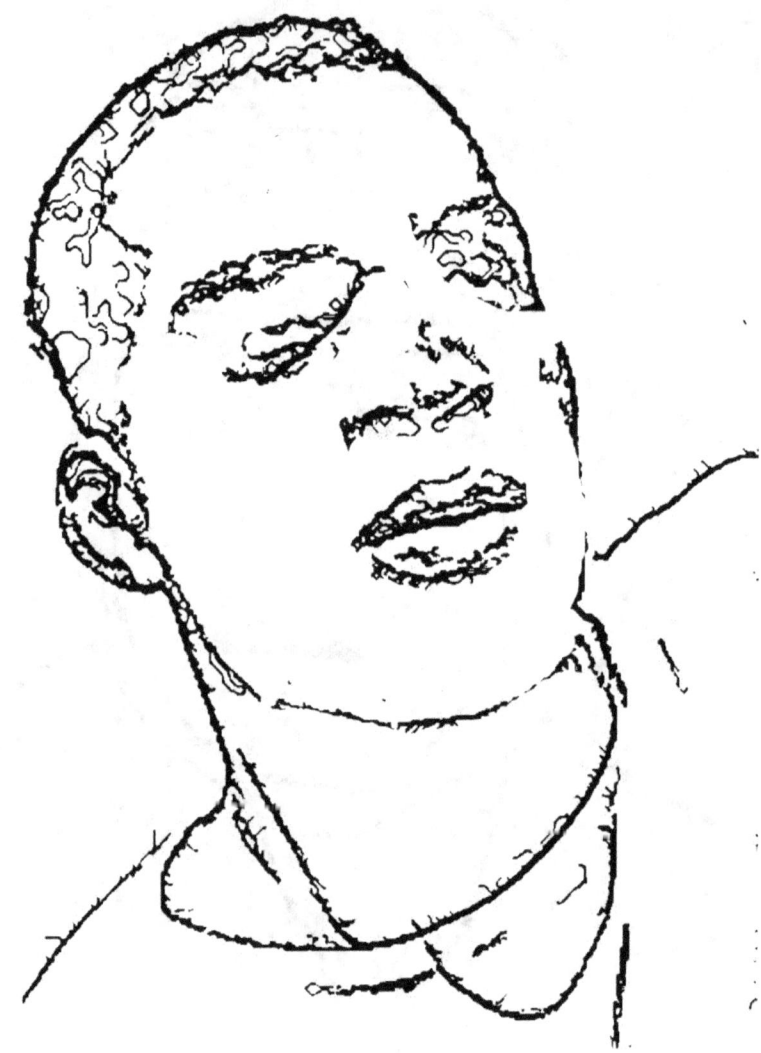

I was a professional football player and the first African American to sign a contract with an NFL team, post-World War II. After my football career I became a police officer.

Toni Cade Bambara

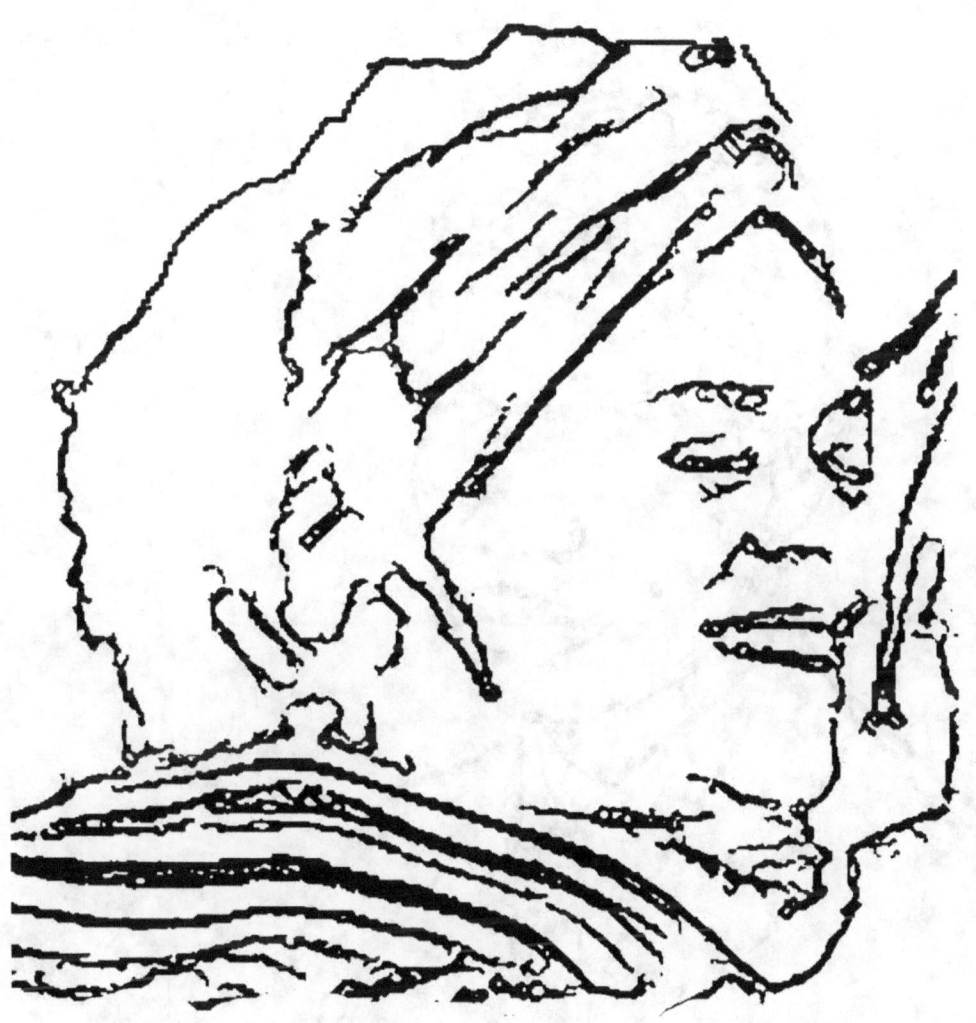

I was an author, college professor, social activist, and documentary film-maker. I wrote, a book titled, "Those Bones Are Not My Child."

Medgar Wiley Evers

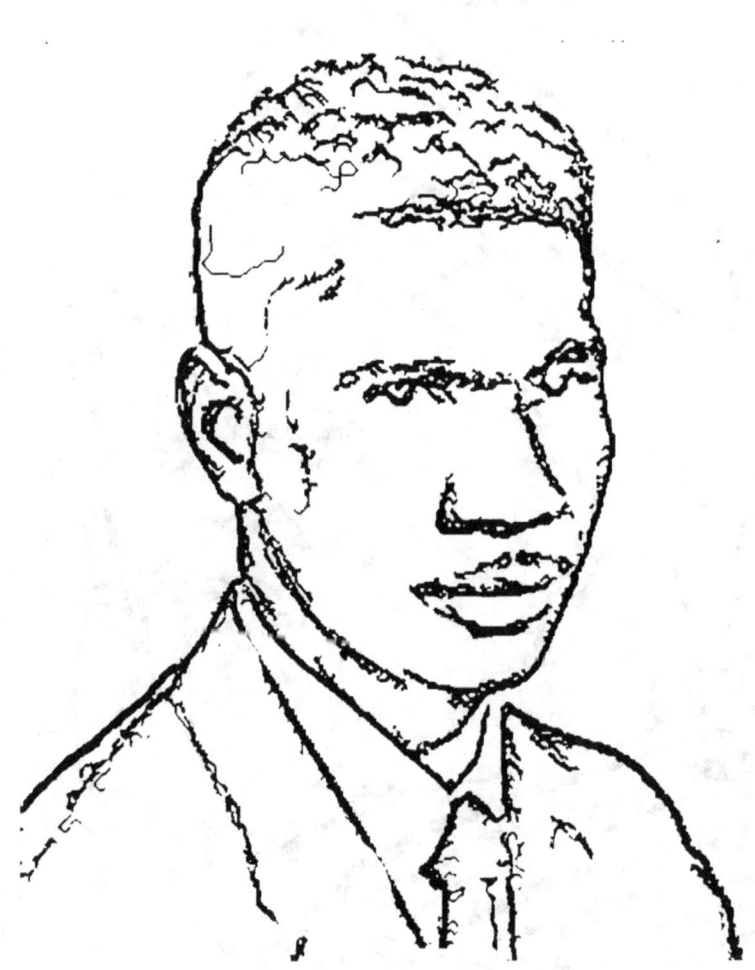

I was a civil rights activist. By fighting to end segregation, I helped overturn segregation at the University of Mississippi and worked with the NAACP as a field secretary.

Michelle Obama

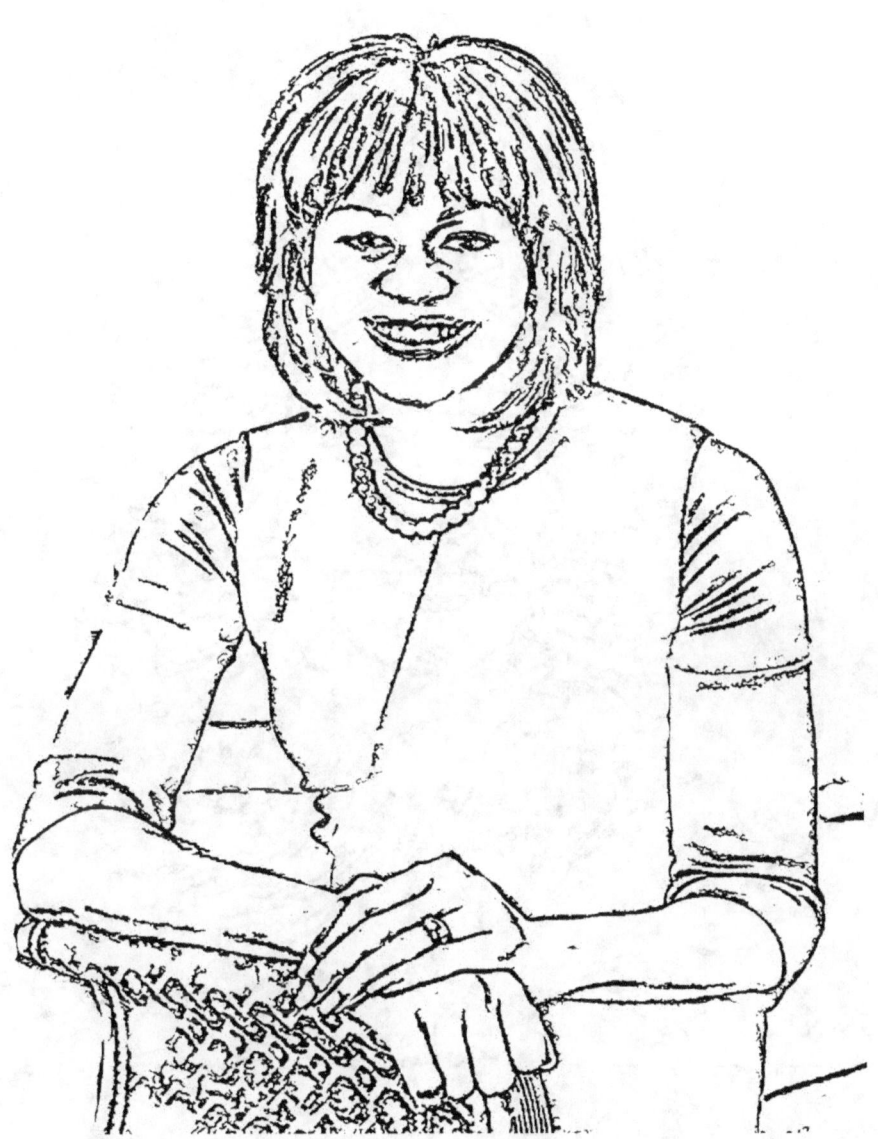

I am First Lady of the Unite States, a lawyer, and writer. I graduated from Harvard Law School. I advocate on behalf of military families and promote good eating habits to help fight obesity. I initiated "Let's Move!" to help reverse the 21st century trend of childhood obesity.

Matthew Henson

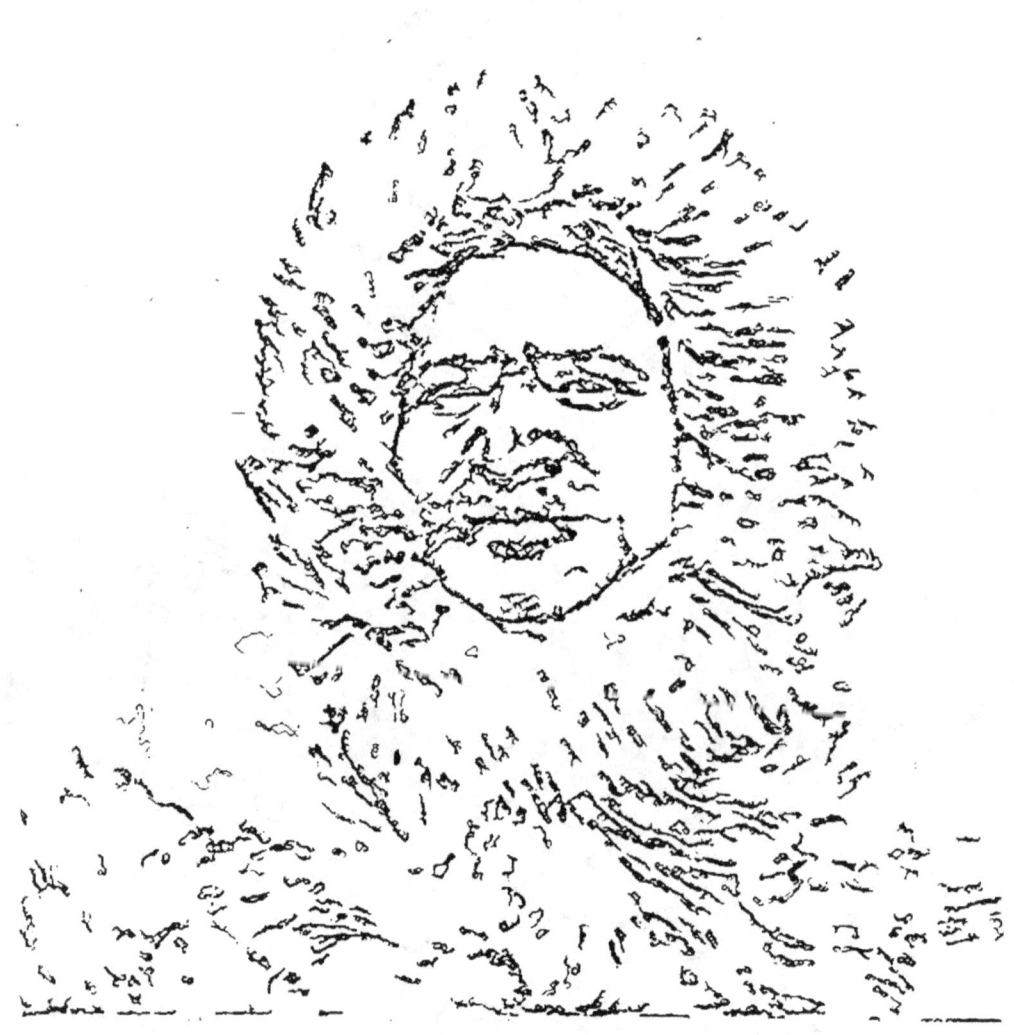

I was an explorer, the first African American Arctic Explorer. I completed a total of six voyages and eighteen expeditions, which took me almost 23 years.

Fritz Pollard

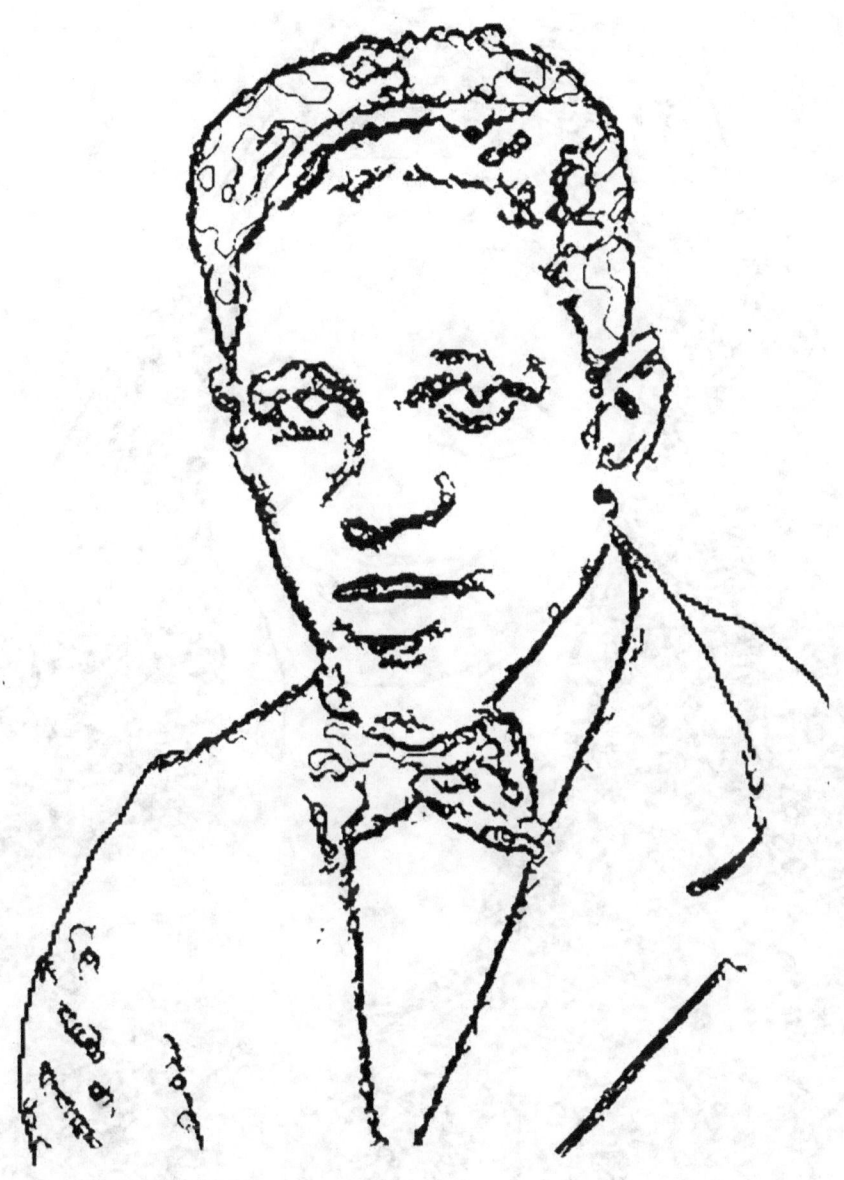

I was a football running back and the first African American head coach in the NFL. In 1920, I was one out of two; to be the first African Americans in the NFL. In the 30s I founded the Brown Bombers" my own professional football team.

Ethel Waters

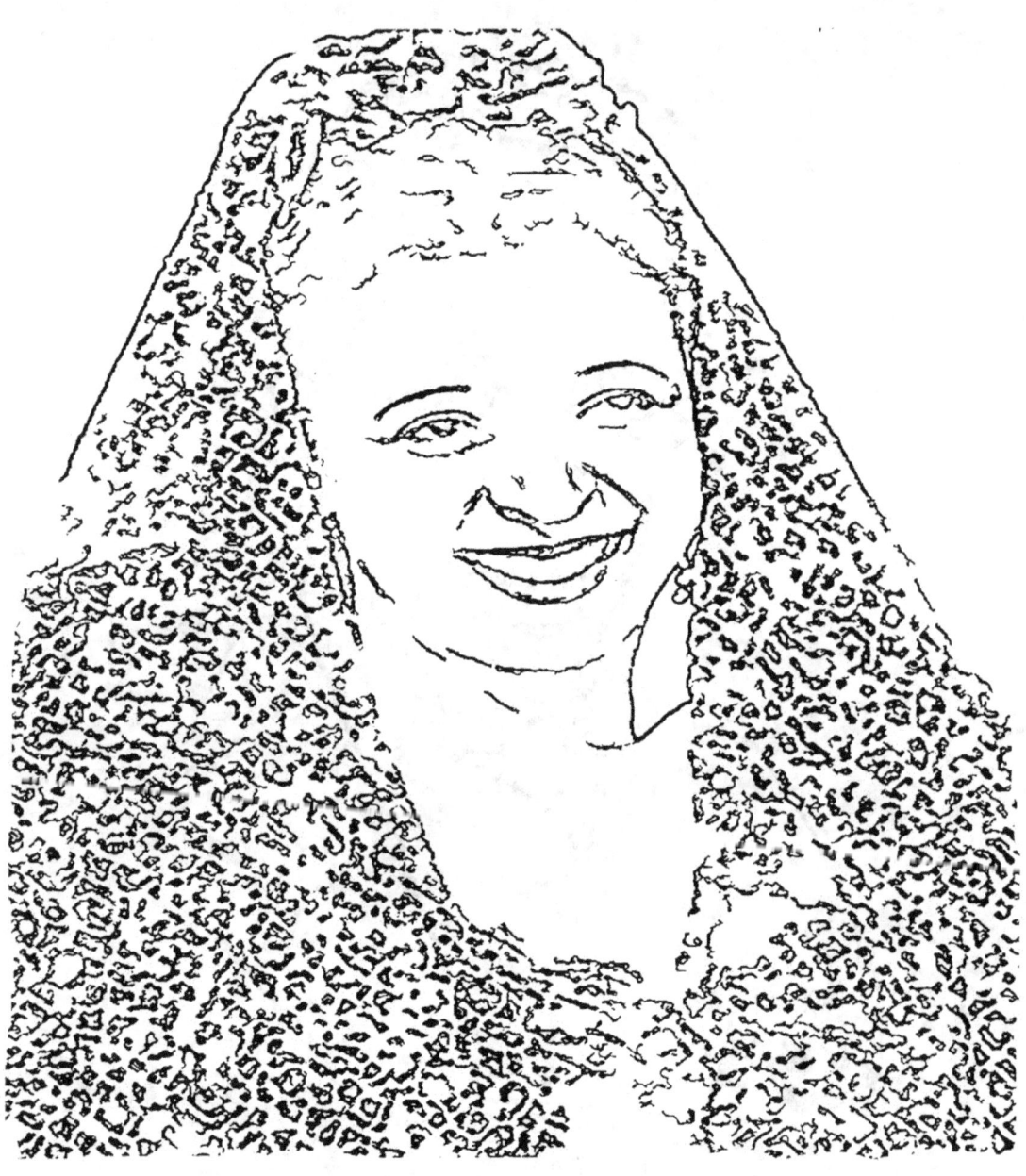

I was an actress, jazz, blues, and gospel singer. I was the first African American woman to be nominated for an Emmy Award and the second African American to be nominated for an Academy Award.

President Obama – 44th President

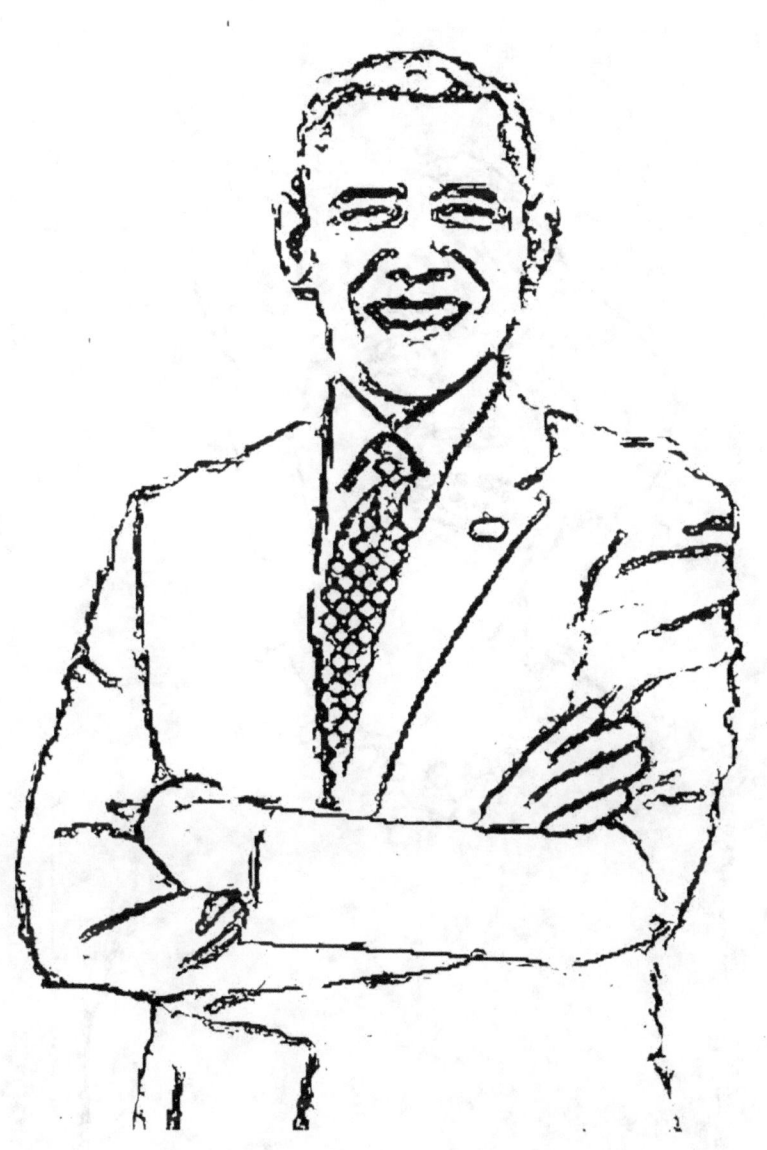

I am the 44th President of the U.S. and an attorney. I am the first African American to hold the highest office in the United States; President and winning two terms. Before becoming president, I served as a community organizer, a civil rights attorney, and taught constitutional law. Then I became an U.S. Senator for the State of Illinois. In 2009, I received the Nobel Peace Prize.

Zora Neale Hurston

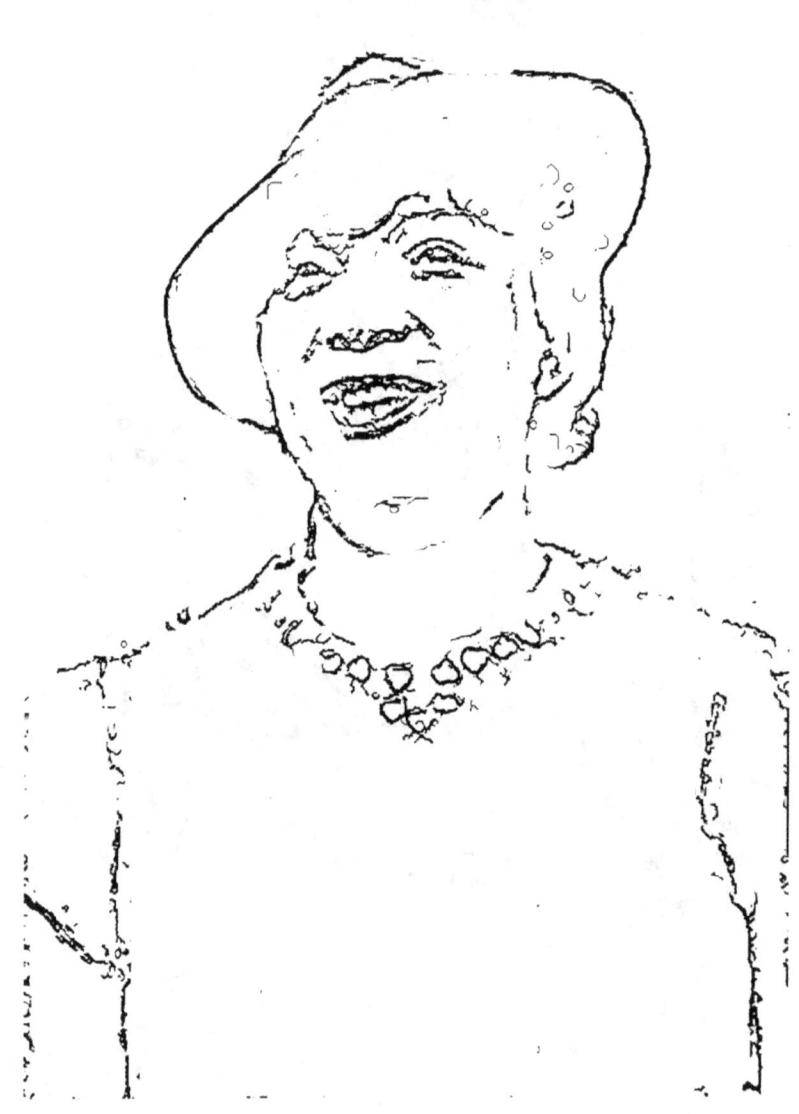

I was an author, anthropologist, and folklorist. In 1928, I wrote an essay titled, "How it Feels to be Colored Me." I co-founded the Howard University student newspaper; "The Hilltop" and wrote the novel, "Their Eyes Were Watching God."

Lucy Diggs Slowe

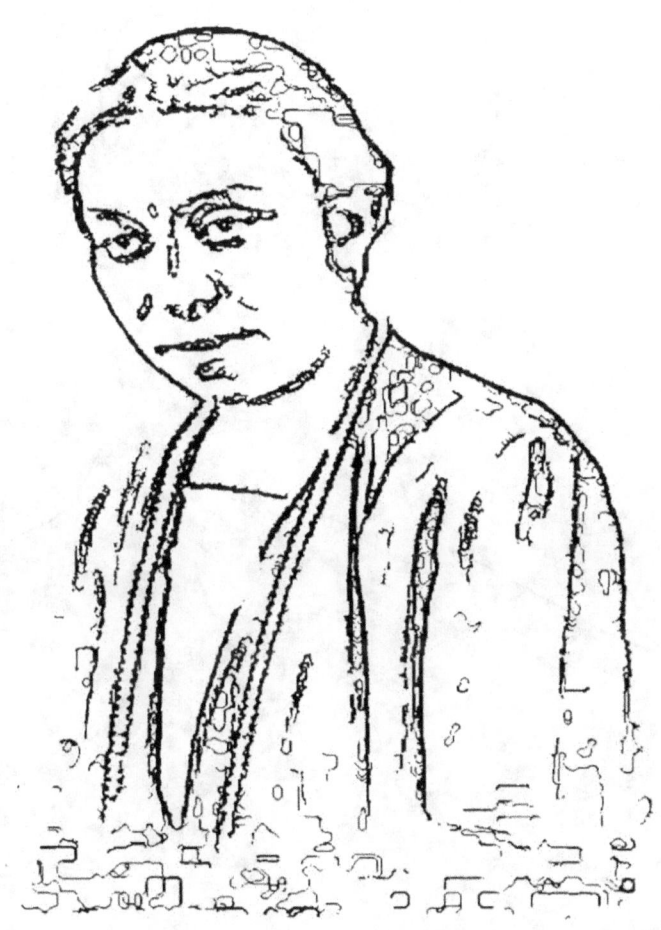

I was a tennis champion in 1917, in which I won the major sports' title. I was one of the original founders of the "Alpha Kappa Alpha Sorority." In 1922, I was the first "Dean of Women" at Howard University, in which I served for 15 years. I had many "first" moments in my lifetime.

Garrett Morgan

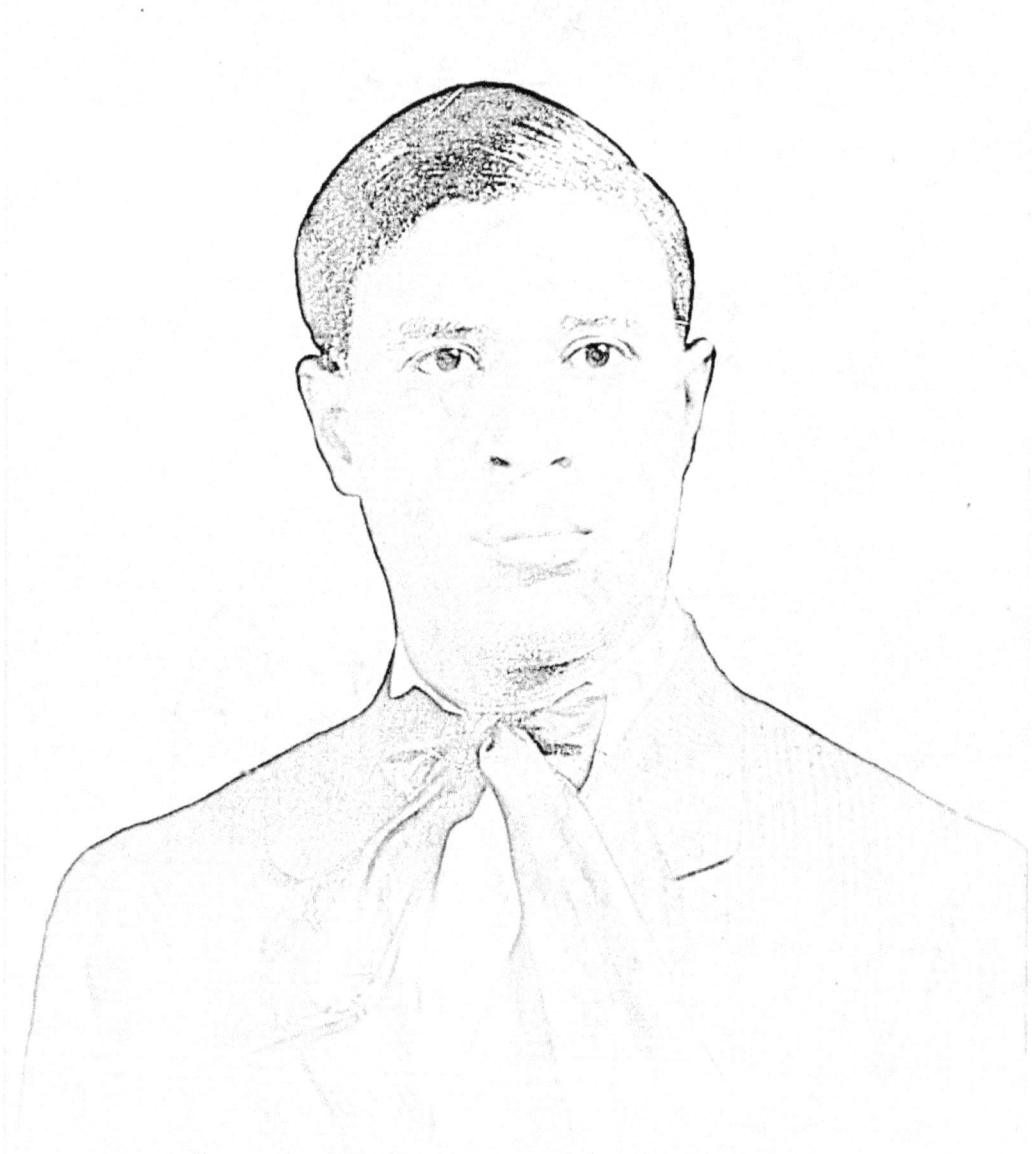

I was an inventor and community leader. I invented the traffic light, a chemical for hair-straightening, and the gas mask. In 1916, the gas mask was used to rescue workers trapped in a tunnel beneath Lake Erie.

James Derham

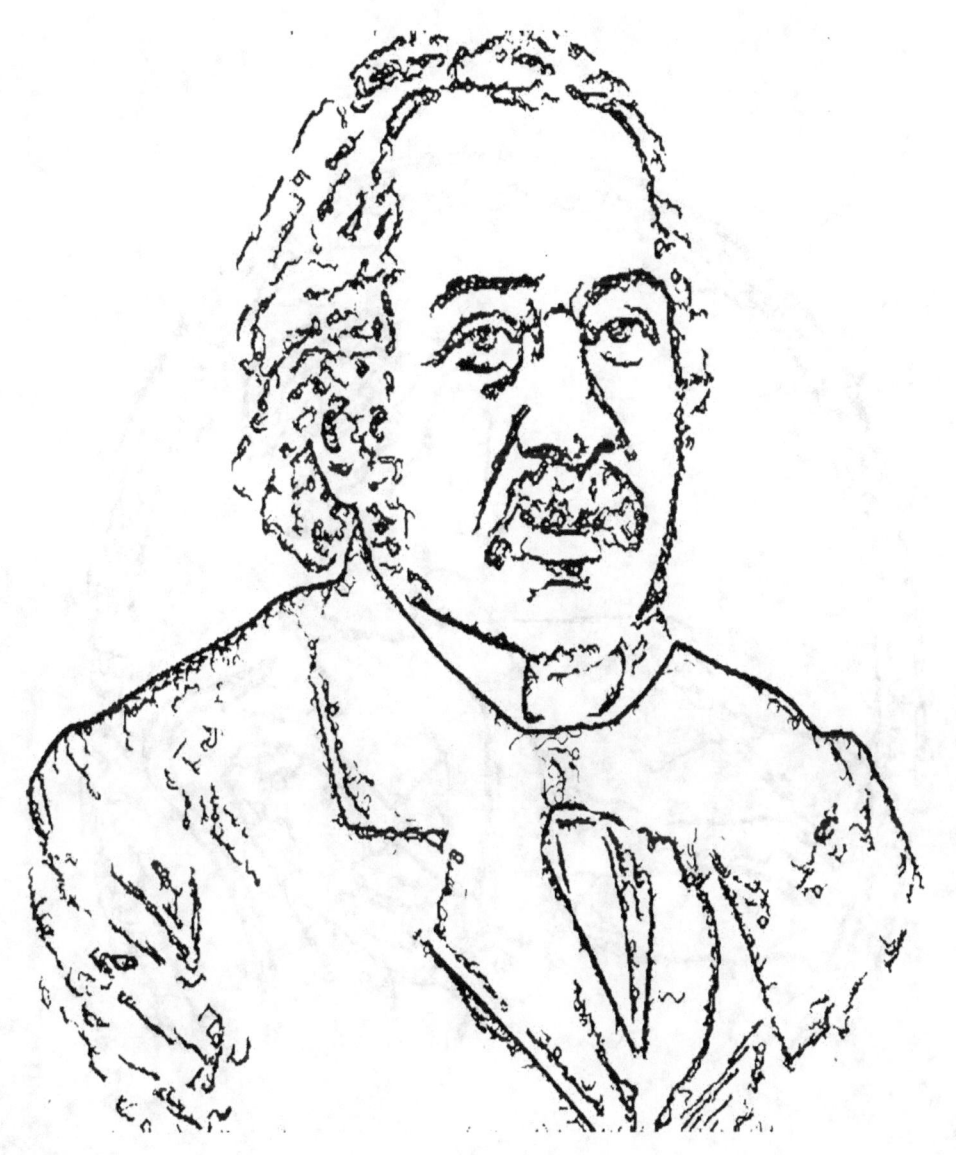

I was a physician. I was born into slavery and was owned by several doctors. I was the first African American to be considered a doctor even though I never received an M.D. degree. I was also the first African American to practice medicine in the U.S.

Phillis Wheatley

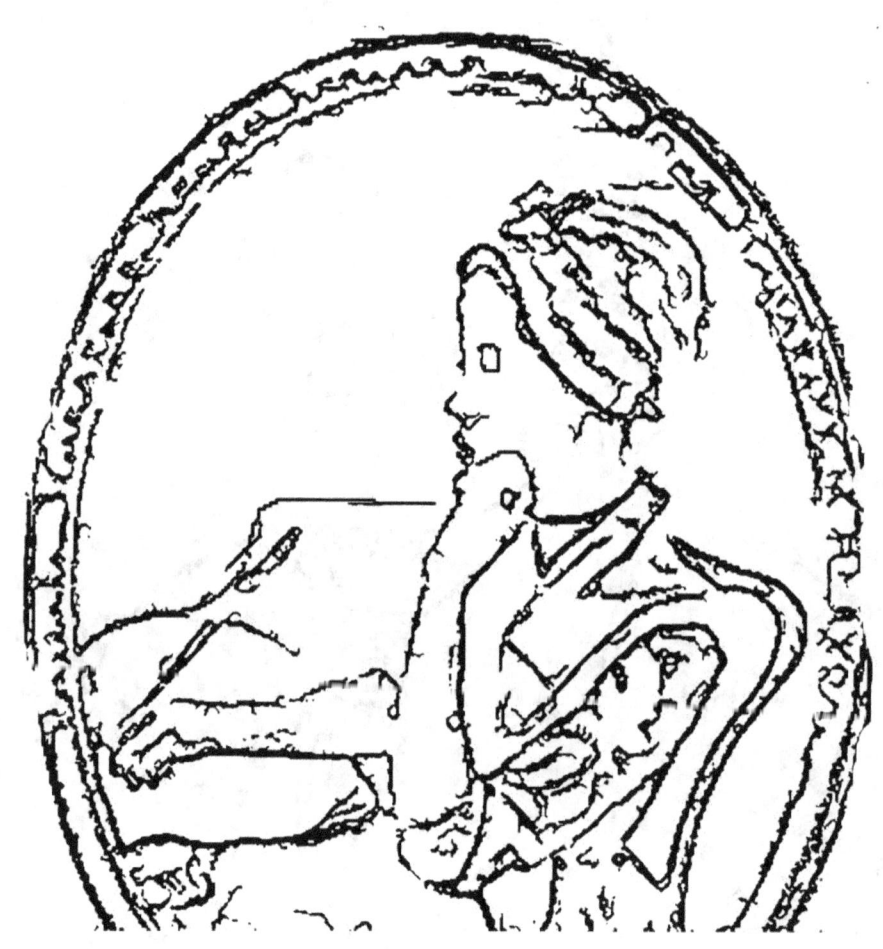

I was an author, poet, and the first African American woman to get published. My writing talent was admired by white colonist. They did not believe an African slave could write such great poetry.

Sadie Alexander

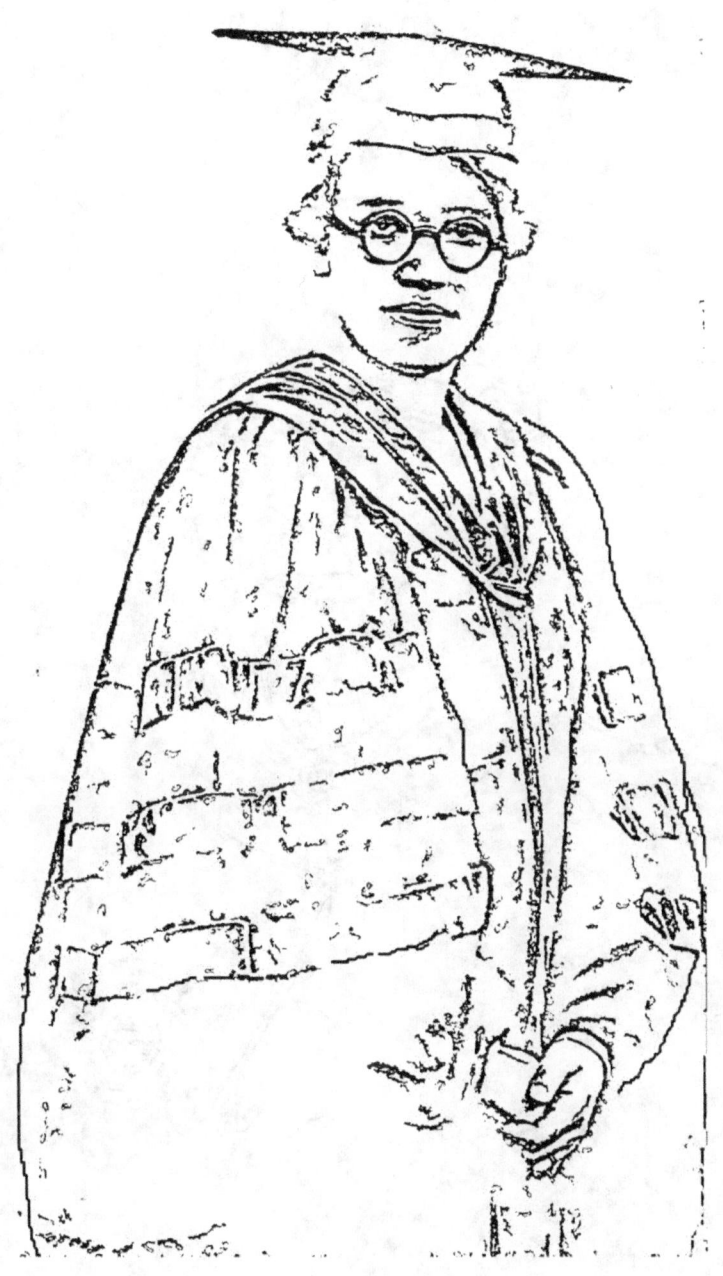

I was an attorney and the first African American to receive a PHD. I was the first woman to receive a law degree from the University of Pennsylvania Law School and the first African American to be appointed as Assistant City Solicitor for the City of Philadelphia. I come from a family of "first" African American achievers.

Granville Woods

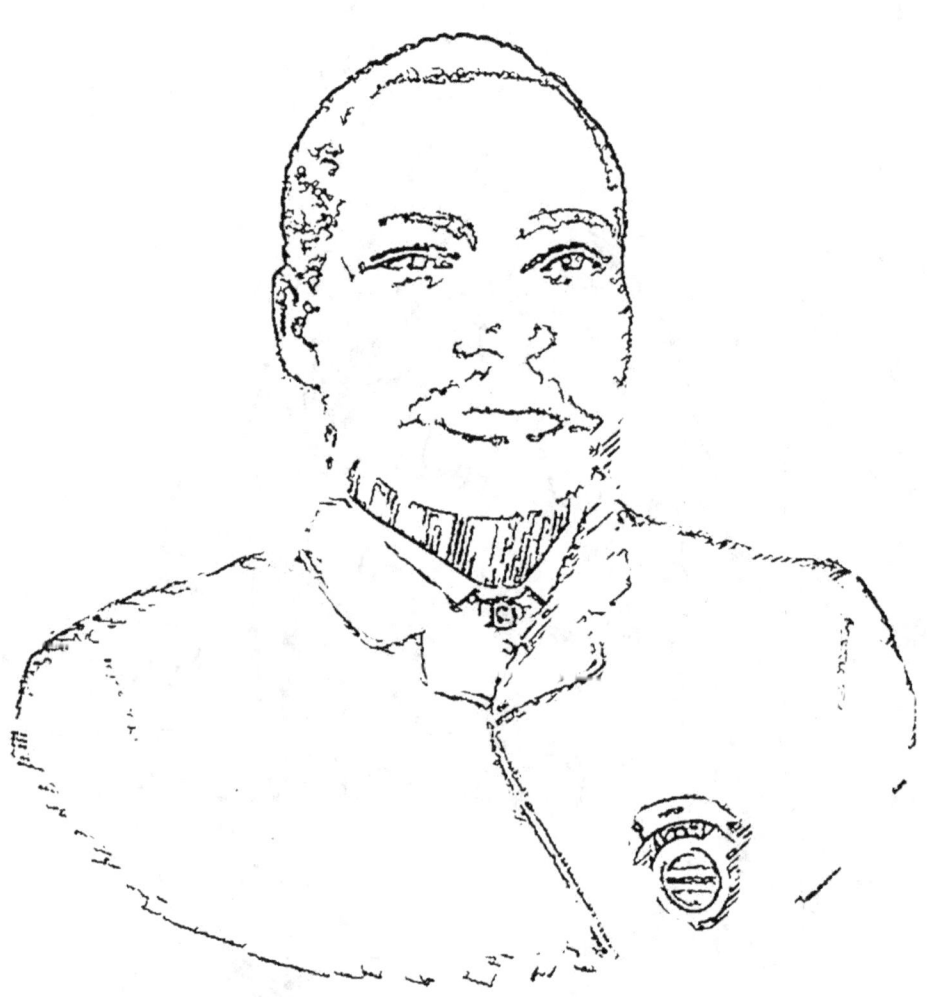

I was an inventor and had over fifty patents. I was a self-taught mechanical and electrical engineer and worked mostly on trains and streetcars. In 1885, I invented an apparatus, a combination of a telephone and telegraph. It was called a "telegraphony".

Martin Luther King, Jr.

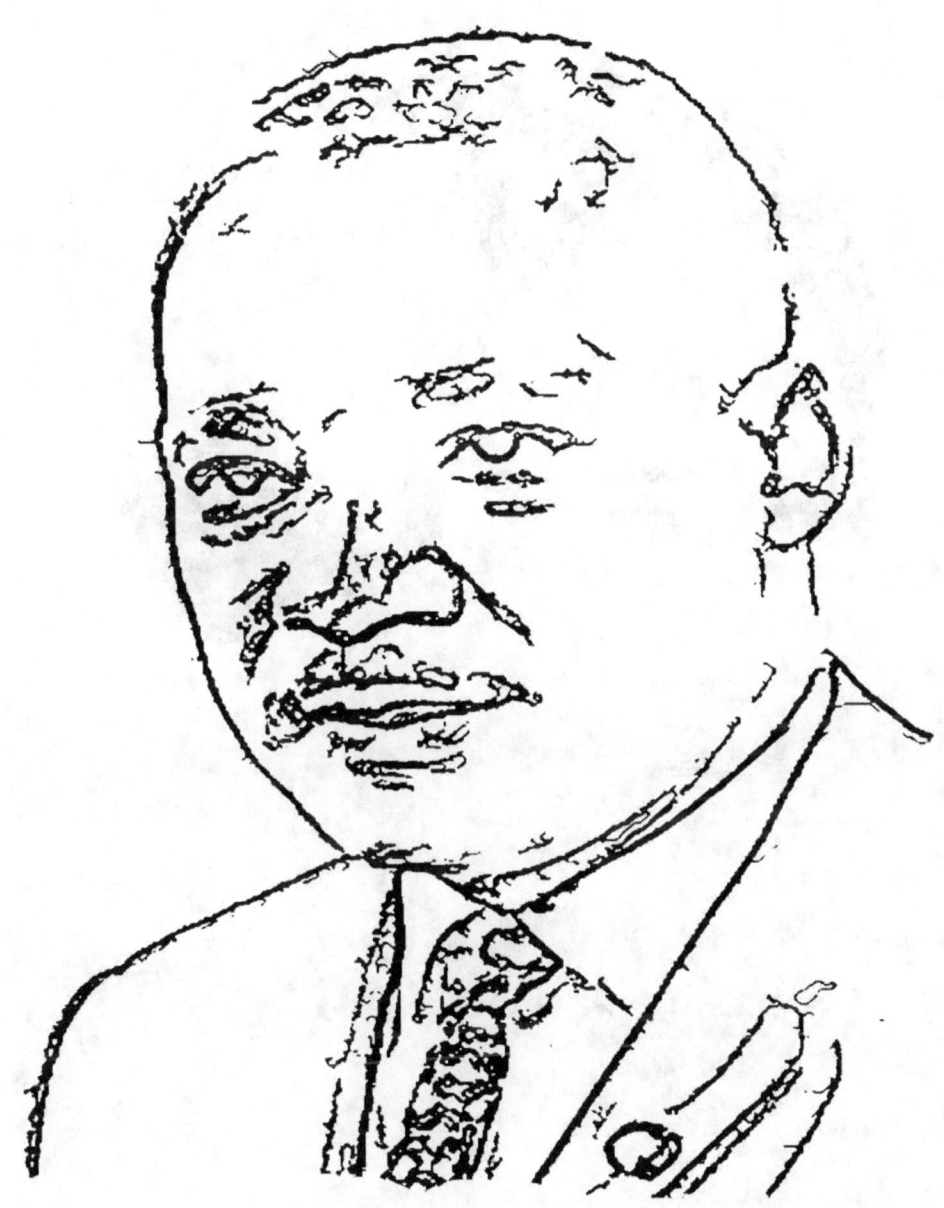

I was a Baptist minister, civil rights leader, and a civil rights activist. I was well-known for my leadership in the African American Civil Rights Movement. I was known throughout the world for my use of nonviolent civil disobedience. In 1963, I delivered my famous speech "I Had a Dream" at the "March on Washington".

Lyda Newman

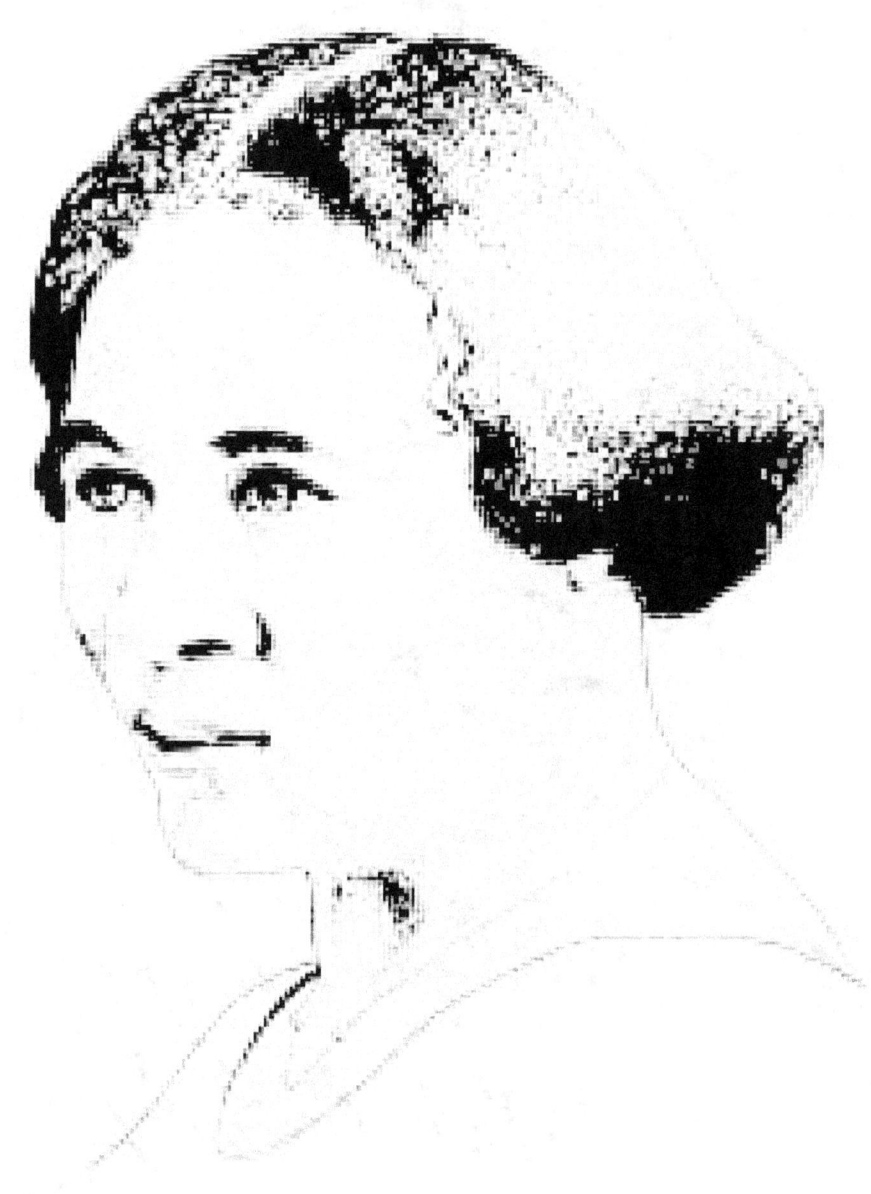

I was an inventor, hairdresser, and a women's activist. I created a new design for the hairbrush. I helped organized an African American branch of the Woman Suffrage Party, which fought for women's right to vote.

Colin Powell

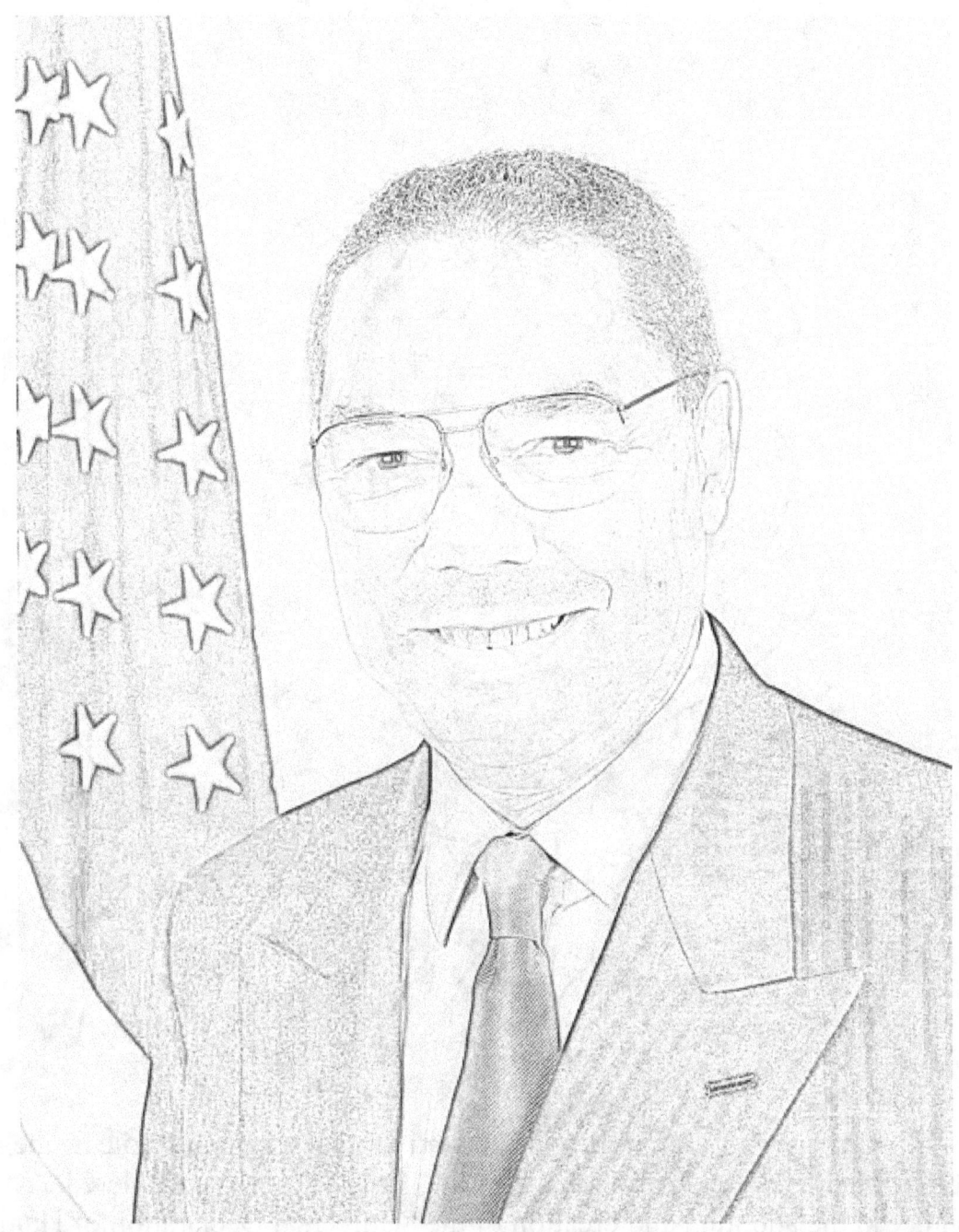

I was the former U.S. Secretary of State and a retired four-star general in the U.S. Army. I served as U.S. Secretary of States under President George W. Bush, from (2001-2005). I also served 35 years in the U.S. Army and served on the Joint Chiefs of Staff.

Ralph Bunche

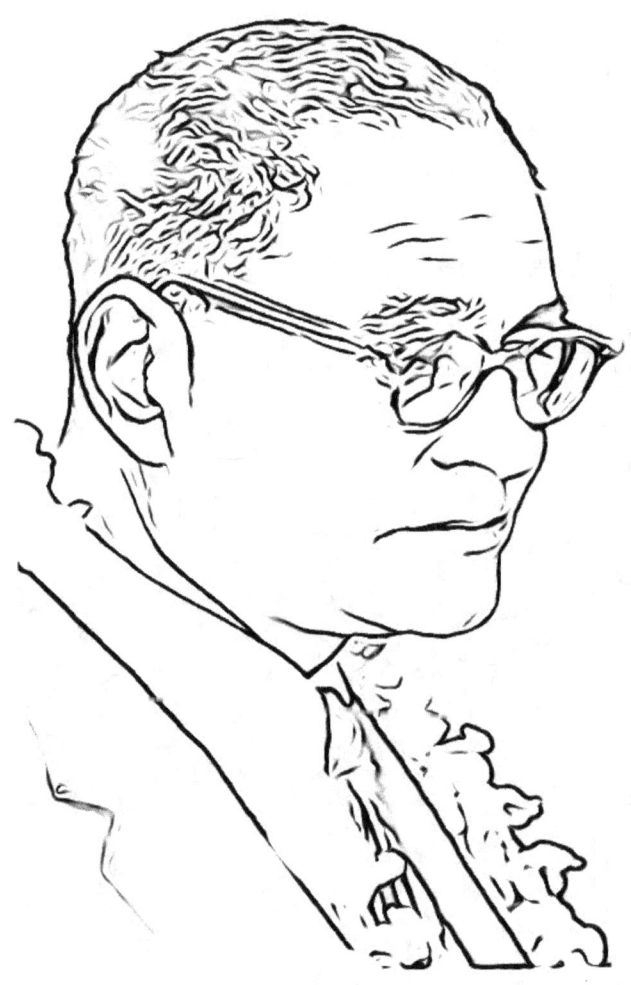

I was a political scientist, diplomat, and academic. I played a major role as the mediator during the 1940s Arab-Israeli conflict. In 1945, I was considered a contributory in the adoption and creation of the "Universal Declaration of Human Rights" during the "Charter Conference" of the UN.

Mary Kenner

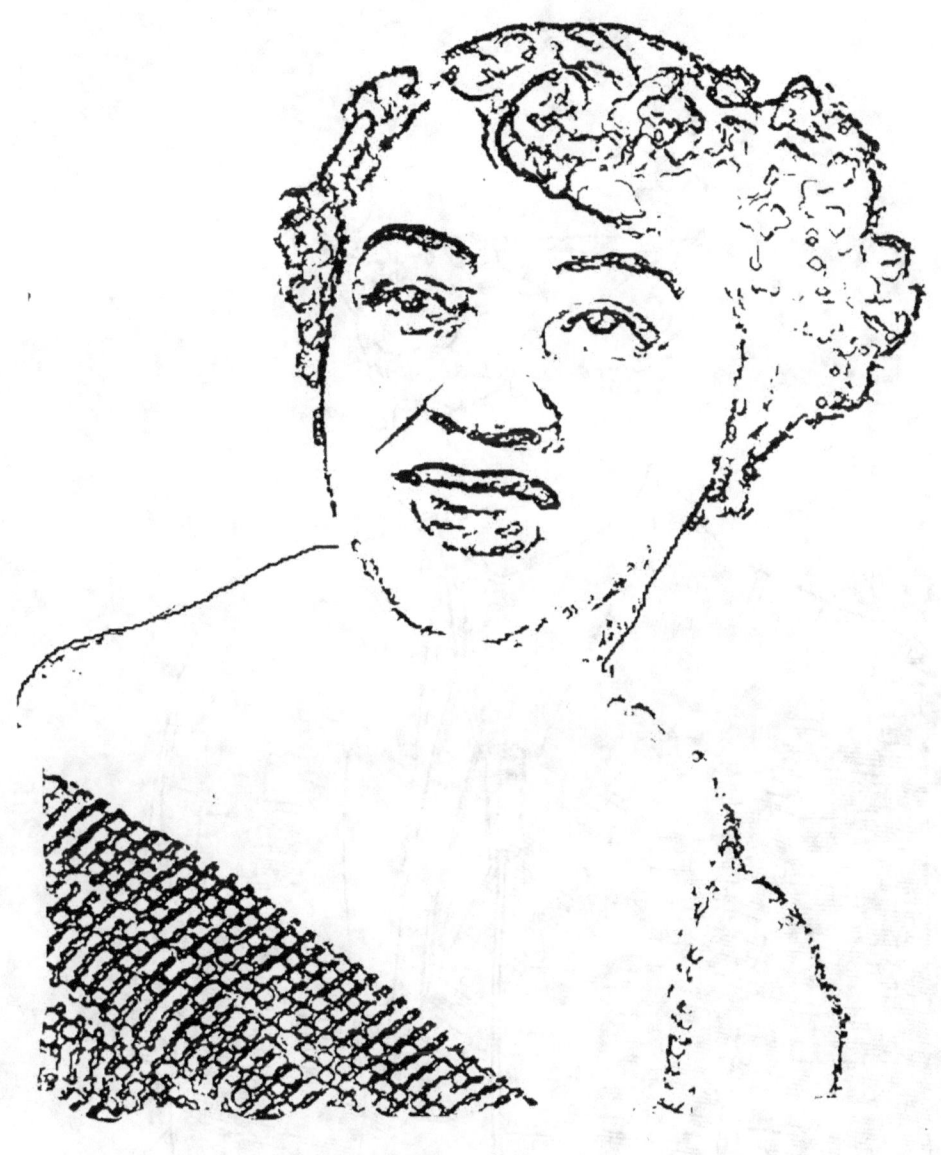

I was an inventor and invented an improved toilet tissue roll holder. I also had other inventions with my sister Mary Davidson.

Malcolm X

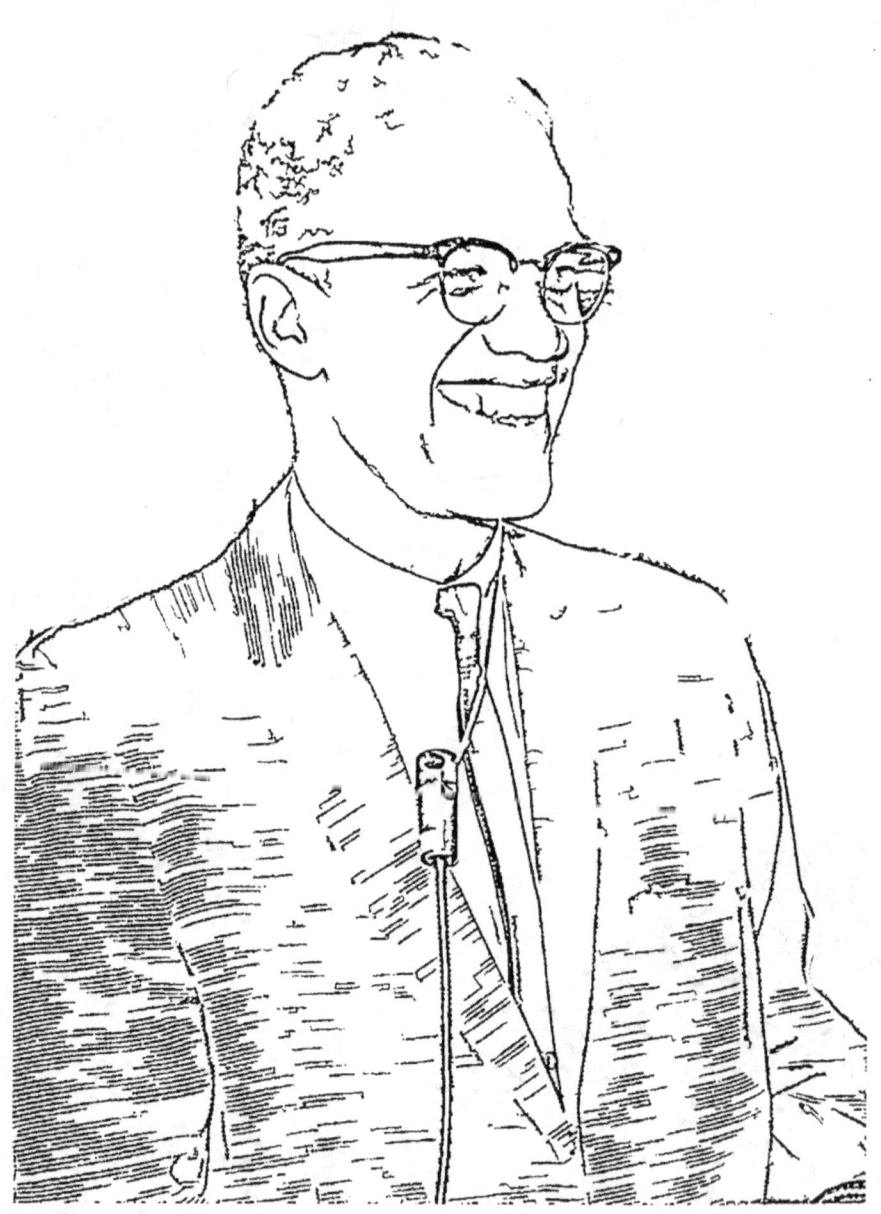

I was a human rights activist and a Muslim minster. I was considered a courageous advocate by those who admired me because I fought for the rights of African Americans.

Jersey Joe Walcott

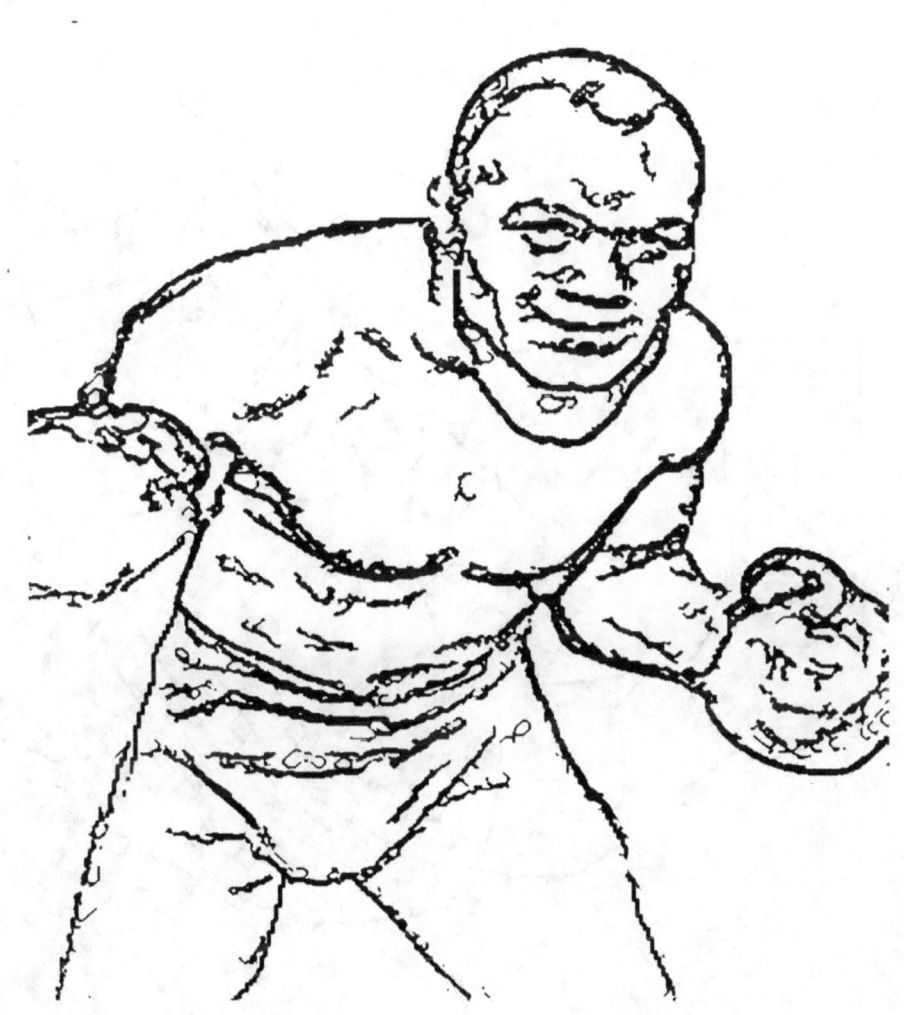

I was a boxer and my birth name was Arnold Cream. I was the oldest man to win the title of the world's heavyweight, at the age of 37. I broke the record when I fought Joe Louis in 1947. In 1971, I was the first African American to be elected as Sheriff in Camden County.

Nancy Green

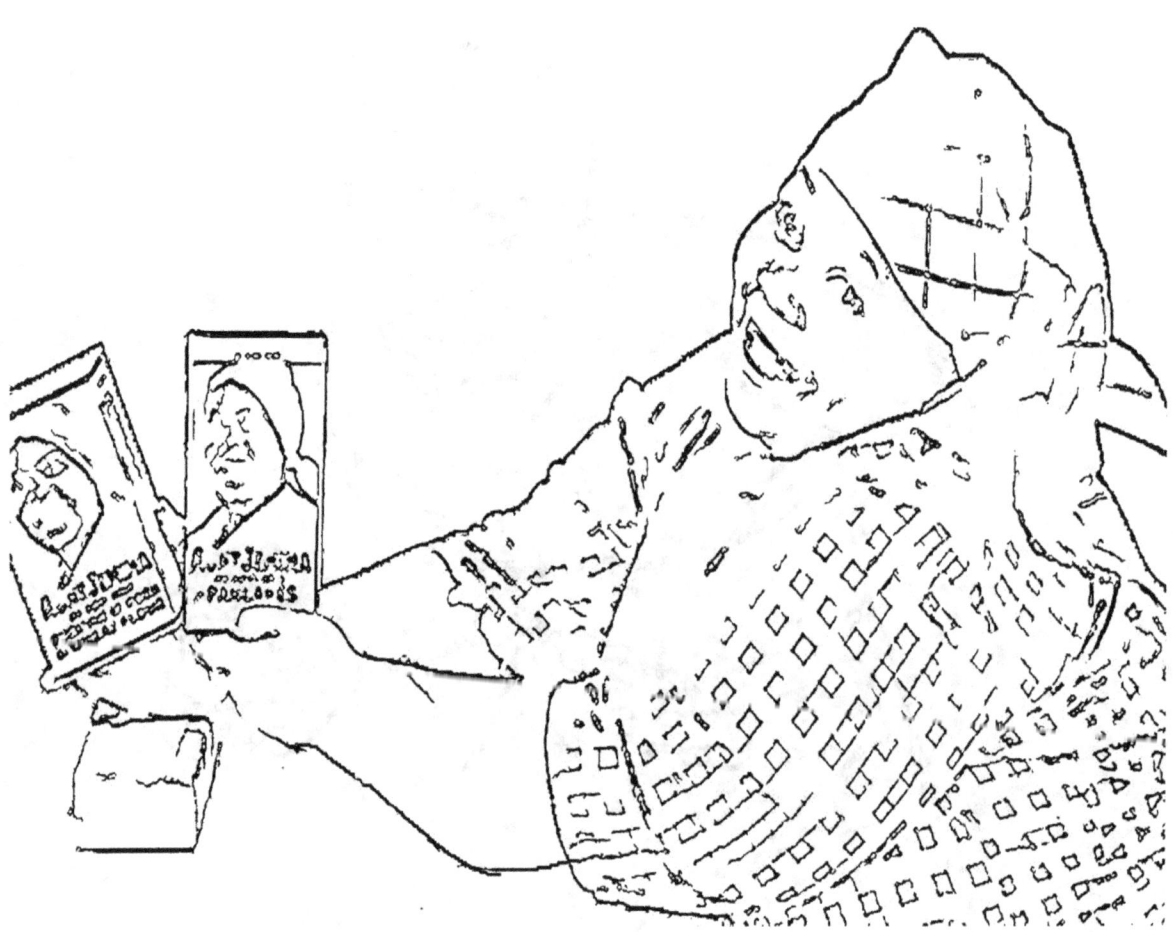

I was a cook, activist, and storyteller. I was hired in 1890 as the model of "Aunt Jemima", which was a name from a minstrel show. I was offered a lifetime contract to portray Aunt Jemima and promote the pancake mix.

Shirley Chisholm

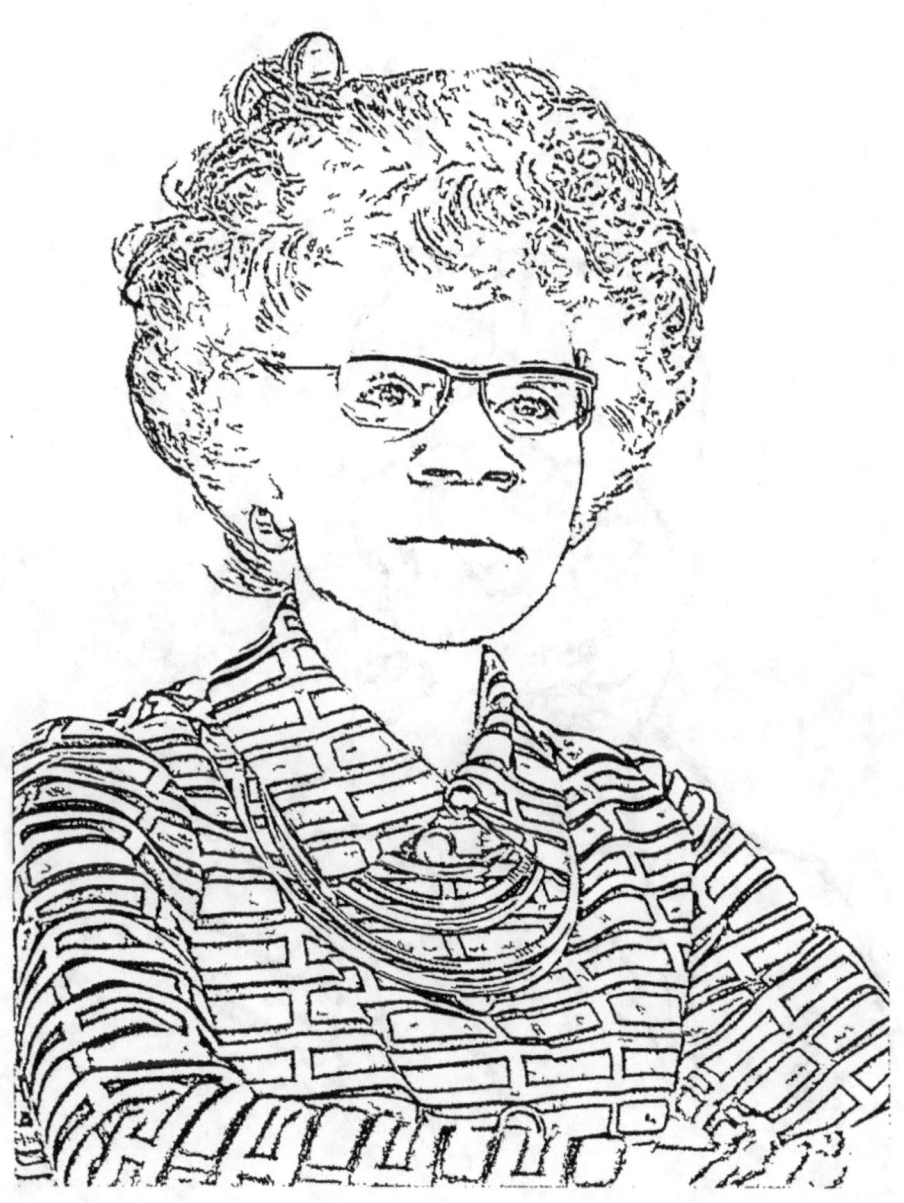

I was a politician, an author, educator, and the first African American woman to be elected Congresswoman. I was the first African American candidate of a major party for President of the U.S. Also, the first woman to run for the presidential nomination of the Democratic Party.

Lucille Hegamin

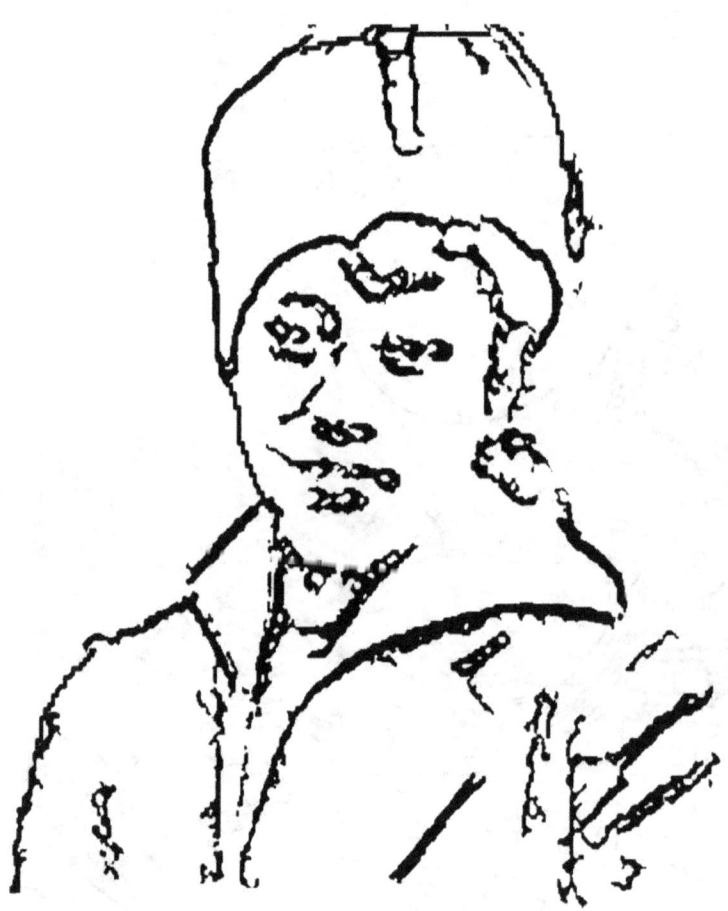

I was an entertainer, blues recording artist, and singer. My record labels included, "Black Swan", "Paramount", and "Arto"; just to name a few. When I retired from singing I became a nurse.

Mamie Smith

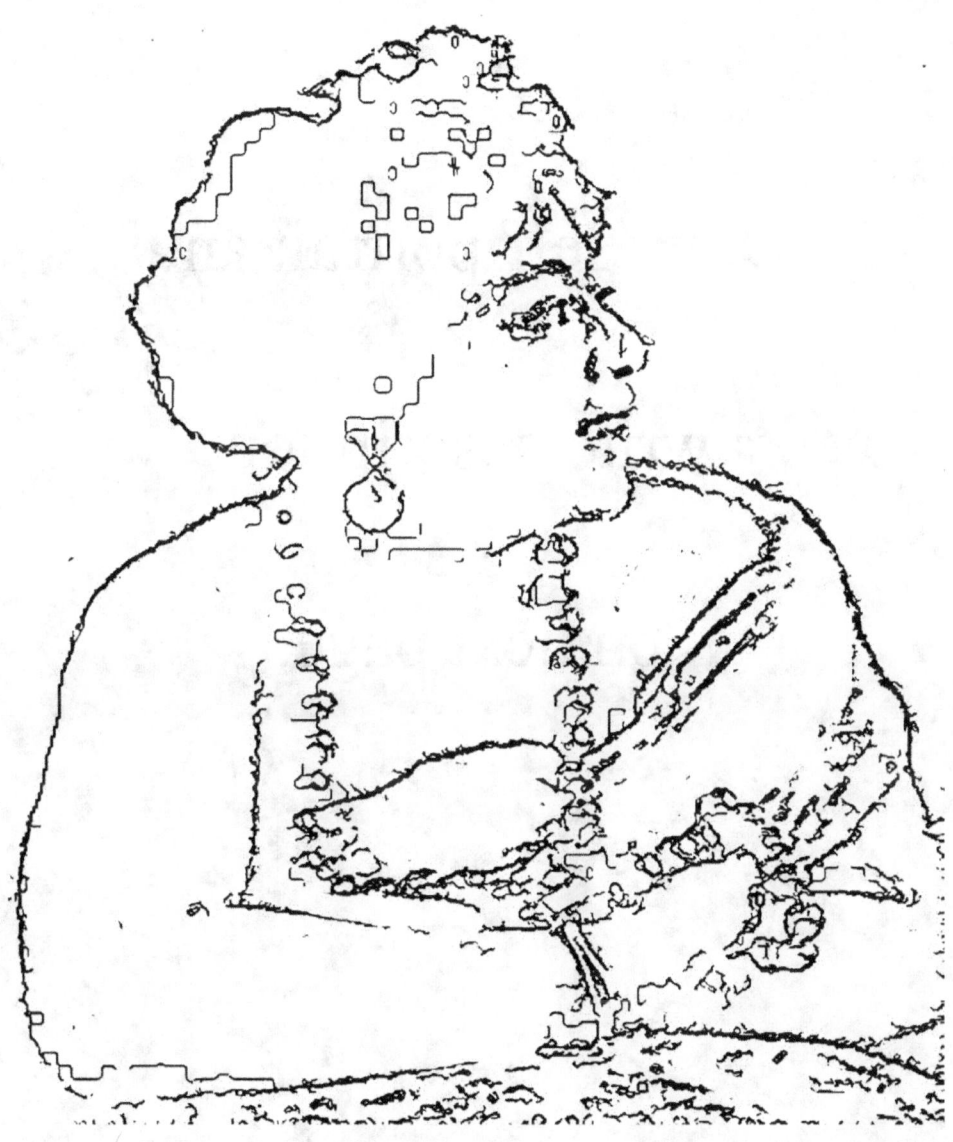

I was a vaudeville singer, actress, pianist, and dancer. In the 1920s I was the first African American to record vocal blues. As a vaudeville singer I performed jazz and blues.

Who Am I?

Draw self-portrait and

write description

on next page.

Name